Christianity

Elaine Baker

Acknowledgements

The author and publisher would like to thank the following for providing the pictures for reproduction:

Ms A I 6 St Matthew, *Book of Kells*	By courtesy of Trinity College, Dublin / Bridgeman Art Library, London.
Madonna and Child with Saints	By courtesy of the National Gallery, London / Bridgeman Art Library, London.
Baptism of Christ	By courtesy of the National Gallery, London / Bridgeman Art Library, London.
Paumgartner Altarpiece	By courtesy of Alte Pinakothek, Munich / Bridgeman Art Library, London.
The Pietà	By courtesy of St Peter's, Rome / Bridgeman Art Library, London.
The Census at Bethlehem	By courtesy of the Musées Royaux des Beaux-Arts de Belgique, Brussels / Giraudon / Bridgeman Art Library, London.
The Supper at Emmaus	By courtesy of the National Gallery, London / Bridgeman Art Library, London.
The Finding of the Young Saviour in the Temple	By courtesy of the Birmingham City Museums and Art Gallery / Bridgeman Art Library, London.
The Yellow Christ	By courtesy of the Albright Knox Art Gallery, Buffalo, New York / Bridgeman Art Library, London.
The Resurrection, Cookham	By courtesy of the Tate Gallery, London / Bridgeman Art Library, London.
The Sacrament of the Last Supper	© Demart Pro Arte BV / DACS 1995 / Bridgeman Art Library, London.
Coventry Cathedral – Baptistry Window	By permission of the Bursar, Coventry Cathedral / Bridgeman Art Library, London.

Folens allows photocopying of pages marked 'copiable page' for educational use, providing that this use is within the confines of the purchasing institution. Copiable pages should not be declared in any return in respect of any photocopying licence.

Folens books are protected by international copyright laws. All rights are reserved. The copyright of all materials in this book, except where otherwise stated, remains the property of the publisher and author. No part of this publication may be reproduced, stored in a retrieval system, or transmitted, in any form or by any means, for whatever purpose, without the written permission of Folens Limited.
This resource may be used in a variety of ways. However, it is not intended that teachers or children should write directly into the book itself.

Elaine Baker hereby asserts her moral rights to be identified as the author of this work in accordance with the Copyright, Designs and Patents Act 1988.

Editor: Andy Brown   Layout artist: Patricia Hollingsworth   Illustrations: Elaine Baker
Cover images: Bridgeman Art Library/Philippa Kingston and Eilidh Weir
Cover design: Gordon Davies of Moss Davies Dandy Turner Ltd

© 1995 Folens Limited, on behalf of the author.

Every effort has been made to contact copyright holders of material used in this book. If any have been overlooked, we will be pleased to make any necessary arrangements.

First published 1995 by Folens Limited, Dunstable and Dublin.
Folens Limited, Albert House, Apex Business Centre, Boscombe Road, Dunstable, LU5 4RL, England.

Printed in Great Britain.

Contents

Ms A I 6 St Matthew, *Book of Kells*	4
Duccio di Buoninsegna – *Madonna and Child with Saints*	6
Piero della Francesca – *Baptism of Christ*	8
Albrecht Dürer – Paumgartner Altarpiece	10
Michelangelo Buonarroti – *The Pietà*	12
Pieter Brueghel the Elder – *The Census at Bethlehem*	14
Michelangelo Caravaggio – *The Supper at Emmaus*	16
William Holman Hunt – *The Finding of the Young Saviour in the Temple*	18
Paul Gauguin – *The Yellow Christ*	20
Stanley Spencer – *The Resurrection, Cookham*	22
Salvador Dali – *The Sacrament of the Last Supper*	24
Coventry Cathedral – Baptistry Window	26
Copiable page – A triskele pattern	28
Copiable page – A street scene	29
Copiable page – A family shield	30
Copiable page – A door-frame pattern	31
Glossary	32

Book of Kells

Time Line

AD 598	King Ethelbert of Kent is converted to Christianity. The bishopric of Canterbury is founded.
627	King Edwin of Northumbria and his Anglo-Saxon followers convert to Christianity.
635	Islam begins its military expansion.
680	Christianity is preached on the Continent by Anglo-Saxon missionaries.
711	Moslems arrive from North Africa to begin the conquest of Spain.
768	Charlemagne becomes King of the Franks.
774	Charlemagne defeats the Lombards and makes himself their king.
789	According to the *Anglo-Saxon Chronicles*, the first Vikings attack England.
c.799	Saxons in north-eastern Germany submit to Charlemagne.
c.805	Ireland is invaded by Vikings from Norway.
800	Charlemagne is crowned Emperor of the Romans by Pope Leo III.
814	The death of Charlemagne.
c.840	Norwegian Vikings found Dublin in Ireland.
c.865	Full-scale invasion of England by the Danes.
871	Alfred the Great becomes King of Wessex.
c.1000	North-American coast is reached by Norwegian Vikings.

Ms A I 6 St Matthew, Book of Kells *c.AD 800*. By courtesy of Trinity College, Dublin / Bridgeman Art Library, London.

QUESTIONS ? ? ? ? ? ? ? ?

1. Saint Matthew was one of the four evangelists. Who were the others? What does the word 'evangelist' mean?

2. Do some research and discover the symbols associated with each of the evangelists.

3. The 'triskele' was a traditional Celtic pattern ('tri' meaning three). Are there any three-sided patterns in this design?

4. Identify any animals or birds in the design.

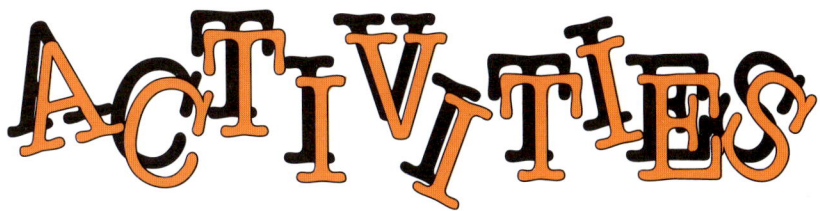

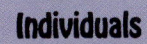

1. Design a border based on the style used in the *Book of Kells*. This could be used to decorate a short prayer or poem. Look carefully at how this border has been constructed and use no more than three colours.

2. Design your own triskele pattern. This could then be put on to pressprint and printed as a repeating pattern on paper or fabric. The pattern on page 28 is an example of a triskele pattern.

3. Find an example of an ancient manuscript. The first capital letter on the page was often drawn much larger than the others and was richly decorated. Choose a short poem, hymn or prayer and write it in the style of an ancient manuscript. The paper can be aged by dabbing cold tea on to it. Enlarge and decorate the first capital letter.

4. Using black paper and coloured tissue paper, design a transparency (like a stained-glass window) based on the style of work shown here. Every member of the group could make a square which could be used as part of a larger transparency.

TECHNIQUES

The earliest medieval manuscripts had been written on papyrus, but the supply of this material ceased owing to the Moslem expansion and control of the Mediterranean lands. European scholars were obliged to use the more costly parchment and so to economise on space the large Roman characters were condensed into smaller compact shapes. Ireland and Anglo-Saxon England developed small letter-writing systems of their own. In the *Book of Kells* there is much use of intricate tracery and ornate borders and rich, stylised designs on parchment. The book has 680 pages, and all but two are in vivid colour, many of them decorated with gold leaf.

Background

BOOK OF KELLS C. AD 800

The *Book of Kells* is justifiably famous for the beauty of its illustrations of religious texts. These were produced in the eighth century by Irish monks, who portrayed the Word of God with highly decorated and stylised designs. Much representational symbolism was used and the designs are extremely intricate and complex.

The script used is sometimes so ornate that it is difficult to read, but the extraordinary patience and skill of the scribes and illuminators who devoted years of their lives to the creation of this masterpiece testifies to their great faith.

Madonna and Child

Time Line

1250 — Robert Grosseteste, the Bishop of Lincoln, protests against the Pope appointing Italians to church posts in England.

1258 — The Mongols destroy Baghdad.

1260 — Chartres cathedral is consecrated.

1264 — Merton College, Oxford is founded. College system starts.

1265 — Simon de Montfort calls the first Parliament.

c.1265 — Marco Polo journeys to the Far East.

1283 — The English conquer Wales.

1290 — The Jews are expelled from Britain.

1291 — The Crusaders are finally driven out of the Holy Land.
Ships from Genoa try to sail around all of Africa.

1296 — Scotland is invaded by the English.

1305 — Clement V becomes the Pope and later moves the papacy to Avignon.

1307–12 — Trial and abolition of the Knights Templar.

1310 — A mechanical clock is perfected.

1314 — The Scots defeat the English at Bannockburn.

c.1320 — Death of Duccio di Buoninsegna.

Madonna and Child with Saints *(triptych)* by Duccio di Buoninsegna c.1260– c.1320.
By courtesy of the National Gallery, London / Bridgeman Art Library, London.

TECHNIQUES

This painting uses gold leaf and tempera on wooden panels. Tempera is a method of painting using powdered colours mixed with the yolk or white of egg instead of oil.

The triptych is composed of three panels, usually of wood, hinged together. The two outer wings with their paintings of saints can be closed over the central panel and are decorated on the reverse. This would stand on the altar.

QUESTIONS?

1. What colour is the background? Would a painted scene be better or is this effective?

2. Would there be some form of decoration on the other side of the panels? What might it be?

3. How many winged angels are there and how many saints? What are the saints' names?

4. Compare this triptych by Duccio with the one by Dürer in this pack. What differences are there in the appearance of the two saints on the side panel and the Virgin Mary?

5. Which triptych do you think is the best? Why?

ACTIVITIES

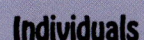

1. Drape a piece of cloth over a chair or stool to produce some interesting folds. Observe these carefully and draw and shade in pencil what is seen. Use the same draped cloth and paint the chair or stool. Compare the results. If possible use a plain piece of cloth so that the shading is not confused by a pattern.

2. Find out about three saints and the symbols associated with them; for example Saint Catherine and the wheel, Saint Andrew and the cross saltire, Saint Francis and some animals. Write a short account of one of their lives and illustrate the account with a portrait of the saint, including their symbol.

3. Look at the circular halo drawn behind the Virgin Mary's head. Draw a large circle and produce a pattern within it that could be used as a halo in this type of painting.

4. Make a clay model of a seated mother and child. The child need not be a baby. The model should be on a clay base. Study pictures of mothers with their children.

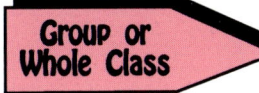

5. Design and make a triptych. Cardboard or wood could be used and the paintings mounted on to this or painted directly on it. As a group, discuss subject matter, treatment and the effect required.

Background

DUCCIO DI BUONINSEGNA c.1260– c.1320

It is thought that Duccio was born around 1260 in Siena, a hill town in Tuscany. He trained as a painter and it is recorded that his first payment was for the painting of 12 chests to hold the public archives for the city. Artists in Siena gained their commissions from the city state, unlike Florentine artists who were mainly employed by wealthy and noble families.

Duccio remained mostly in Siena. This is documented by various payments for civic work and also a succession of legal fines for various misdemeanours including obstruction of a public road and refusal to fight with the civil militia. His reputation as a painter seems to have been unaffected by his legal problems.

When he was commissioned to paint his masterpiece the *Maestà* in 1308, Duccio agreed that he would concentrate solely on this and do no other work and also receive a salary of 16 soldi a day. On 9 June 1311, the huge painted altarpiece was finished and taken in procession to Siena Cathedral. Agnol dio Tura, a chronicler, estimated its total cost to be 3000 gold florins which must make it one of the most expensive pieces of its kind ever to be produced.

Baptism of Christ

Time Line

c.1420 — Piero della Francesca is born in Borgo San Sepolcro, near Florence. Brunelleschi designs and begins to build the dome for the cathedral in Florence.

1431 — Saint Joan of Arc is tried and burned at the stake in Rouen.

1434 — Cosimo de Medici comes to power in Florence. He dominates for the next 30 years.

1453 — The Hundred Years' War ends. Constantinople falls to the Ottoman Empire.

1454 — Printing with movable type is first used.

1455–85 — The Wars of the Roses in England.

1455 — A bible is printed with 42 lines per page by Gutenberg.

1469 — Lorenzo de Medici becomes head of state in Florence.

1472 — Arabic figures are used for numbering book pages.

1479 — Small guns are developed. The idea comes from mobile cannon.

1482–84 — Venice is at war with the rest of Italy.

1484 — Innocent VIII becomes Pope.

1489 — Cyprus is occupied by Venice.

1492 — Piero della Francesca dies in Borgo San Sepolcro.

Background

PIERO DELLA FRANCESCA c.1420–1492

Piero della Francesca was born c. 1420 in the small town of Borgo San Sepolcro, south-east of Florence. In Vasari's *Life of Piero* written in the sixteenth century, it is reported that his father, a tanner and toolmaker named Beredette, died before Piero was born and that his mother, Romana, brought him up.

In 1439 it is known that he was working with Domenico Veneziano in Florence. The city at that time was at the zenith of its power attracting many artists and intellectuals. Piero was influenced by the work around him including the new exciting theories of perspective.

He went on to become a master of perspective himself. He wrote a treatise and also instructed the architect Bramante in the use of perspective.

From 1452 until 1466 he was involved in painting the Arezzo cycle of frescos. He dearly loved his hometown, always returning to it and sometimes depicting it in the background of his paintings. He was elected a town councillor at Borgo San Sepolcro in 1442 and again in 1467, and died there in 1492, having become a famous painter and the town's celebrity.

TECHNIQUES

Piero della Francesca worked in fresco, and on wooden panels using tempera and oils. He used colour in a very structural way, working with a relatively small range of colours, repeating them throughout his compositions to form strong structural links.

Piero portrayed ideal and heroic faces in an austere yet serene way. There are no turbulent emotions on show. He created precise perspective and architectural details alongside some of the most solemn and serene images in Christian art.

ACTIVITIES

Individuals

1. This painting contains some well-observed trees and plants. Use a sketchbook to draw some trees and plants from life. Then turn some of the drawings into an accurate painting.

2. Piero Della Francesca made many studies of perspective, even writing a treatise on the subject called *De Prospettiva Pingendi*. Draw a street scene using simple one-point perspective (page 29 could be used as a starting point).

3. Look at the painting of the dove. Research the different shapes created by birds during flight and create a repeating design which could be used on printed fabric. Think about which colours would be suitable.

4. Look at the face of the central angel on the left. Draw and then paint a quiet, placid, unlined face in the same style. Then draw and paint an older, lined and wrinkled face alongside it as a comparison.

In Small Groups

5. Piero worked with a relatively small range of colours. The blue of the sky is echoed in the angels' robes and wings, the dark green of the trees is repeated not only on the ground but also in the background. Paint a scene with at least three people in it and try to use a soft and limited colour range. Do not use black. Pay particular attention to the balance of the colours.

Baptism of Christ *by Piero della Francesca c.1420–1492. By courtesy of the National Gallery, London / Bridgeman Art Library, London.*

QUESTIONS?

1. Who is baptising Jesus in the painting? Find out who Jesus' parents were and the story of his baptism.

2. Water is being poured on to Jesus' head from a bowl and the dove hovers overhead with wings outstretched. What Old Testament story does a dove also appear in? What is the dove usually regarded as a symbol of?

3. Piero Della Francesca used the town of Borgo San Sepolcro (his birthplace) in the background of this picture. Where is it in the painting?

4. Where are the angels standing in the painting? How many of them are there?

5. Piero della Francesca used a geometry of triangles, horizontals and verticals in this painting. Try to find them.

9

Paumgartner Altarpiece

Time Line

1471	Albrecht Dürer is born on 21 May in Nuremberg, Germany.
1475	The Vatican Library is opened to the public by Pope Sixtus IV. Michelangelo Buonarotti is born.
1482–84	Venice is at war with the rest of Italy.
1486–89	Savonarola preaches in Florence.
1492	Christopher Columbus sails across the Atlantic, discovering America. Rodrigo de Borgia becomes Pope Alexander VI. The death of Lorenzo de Medici.
1494	The Medicis are virtually bankrupt and are driven from Florence.
1497	Savonarola is excommunicated.
1498	Savonarola is burned at the stake as a heretic. Vasco da Gama discovers the sea route to India.
1503–04	Leonardo da Vinci paints the *Mona Lisa*.
1507	Martin Luther is ordained a priest.
1508–12	Michelangelo paints the Sistine Chapel ceiling.
1509	Catherine of Aragon marries Henry VIII. The pocket watch is invented by Peter Henlein.
1516	Sir Thomas More writes *Utopia*. Erasmus edition of the New Testament.
1527	The Reformation. Lutheranism becomes the state religion of Sweden and Denmark.
1528	Albrecht Dürer dies aged 57 on 6 April.

Background

ALBRECHT DÜRER 1471–1528

Albrecht Dürer was born on 21 May 1471 in Nuremberg. His father was a Hungarian goldsmith and Albrecht was the third of 18 children. At an early age he showed signs of his prodigious talent and at the age of 15 he was apprenticed to the Nuremburg painter, Michael Wolgemut.

At the age of 18 he left for the traditional German 'bachelor's year', a time spent wandering from city to city so that life could be fully explored before settling down to family responsibilities. He married Agnes Frey, the daughter of a Nuremburg coppersmith, in 1493.

Dürer travelled to Italy and was greatly influenced by the new Italian masters. On his return home he produced many woodcuts and engravings. These spread his fame and gained him the independence that he craved.

Albrecht Dürer died in 1528 of a fever contracted during a visit to Zeeland, leaving no descendants.

Paumgartner Altarpiece: central panel, the Nativity and Members of the Paumgartner Family; left-hand wing, St George; right-hand wing, St Eustace by Albrecht Dürer 1471–1528.
By courtesy of Alte Pinakothek, Munich / Bridgeman Art Library, London

ACTIVITIES

Individuals

In Small Groups

Group or Whole Class

1. The saints in the outer panels and the Paumgartner family depicted in the centre are shown holding their heraldic shields or banners. Design a shield or banner suitable for your family. Use your family name and the activities that interest you as a basis for your design. Page 30 could be used as a template.

2. The centre panel uses perspective to give a feeling of distance. Use one-point perspective to draw a narrow street. It is not necessary to include people. Page 29 could be used as a starting point.

3. Look at the landscape in the centre of the middle panel. Create a painting of a view through an archway. Use dark colour for the archway surround to lead the viewer into the picture.

4. Draw and paint a version of the Nativity. Decide if any elements of modern dress or buildings should be included, or whether a more traditional approach would be better.

5. Make a clay model of either a figure, a face or the dragon from this picture. Make the figure or dragon lying or kneeling. Pay particular attention to any surface texture or draperies.

QUESTIONS？？？？？？？？？？

1. This altarpiece is a triptych. 'Tri' means three. What might the description triptych refer to with regard to the altarpiece?

2. The side panels of the altarpiece show Saint George, with the slain dragon, and Saint Eustace. Which country is Saint George the patron saint of? Find out about Saint Eustace.

3. The Paumgartner family on the central panel are portrayed with their family shields. How many of them are portrayed? What suggests that they were a wealthy family?

4. What is the baby lying in? Who is holding him?

5. Look at the perspective of the central panel with the upright and diagonal shapes dividing the painting into separate areas. Compare this with the triptych by Duccio. Are they similar?

TECHNIQUES

Dürer excelled at the woodcut technique which was popular in Germany. He drew the designs directly on to soft wood and they were then chiselled out by highly-trained craftsmen. The remaining parts of the block would then be inked and printed on to paper. He used perspective which he learned in Italy to give space and depth to his work.

Dürer, like Leonardo da Vinci, was fascinated by the natural world and experimented and developed in many media. Some of Dürer's greatest works are his copperplate engravings – the technique of woodcut printing allied to ornamental engraving on silver and gold particularly suited his background and style.

11

The Pietà

Time Line

1475 — Michelangelo Buonarroti is born.

1482–84 — Venice is at war with the rset of Italy.

1486–89 — Savonarola preaches in Florence.

1492 — Christopher Columbus sails across the Atlantic and discovers America.

1493 — Columbus returns and Pope Alexander VI divides the newly-found land of America between Spain and Portugal.

1497 — Savonarola is excommunicated.

1498 — Savonarola is burned at the stake as a heretic.
Vasco da Gama discovers the sea route to India.

1503 — Julius II becomes Pope.

1503–04 — Leonardo da Vinci paints the *Mona Lisa*.

1508–12 — Michelangelo paints the Sistine Chapel ceiling.

1510 — The pocket watch is invented by Peter Henlein.

1519 — Leonardo da Vinci dies.
Magellan begins his world voyage.

1527 — The Reformation. Lutheranism becomes the state religion of Sweden and Denmark.

1533–41 — Michelangelo paints *The Last Judgement*.

1550 — First suspension bridge built by Palladio.

1564 — Pencils with a graphite core enclosed in wood appear in Europe.
Births of Shakespeare and Galileo.
Death of Michelangelo.

The Pietà *by Michelangelo Buonarroti 1475–1564. By courtesy of St Peter's, Rome / Bridgeman Art Library, London.*

QUESTIONS ?????????

1. What is the subject of this piece of sculpture?

2. When this sculpture was first shown some people complained that the Virgin Mary looked too young. Does she appear to be the correct age?

3. Every surface on this sculpture is highly polished. Look at the intricate folds. What makes it look as though it is carved from a single piece of marble?

4. Carrara was famous for the purity and whiteness of the marble found there. Why might Michelangelo have chosen this stone for his sculpture?

5. Michelangelo was also a painter. Where did he paint a famous ceiling? What was its subject?

ACTIVITIES

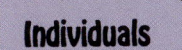

1. Michelangelo carved wonderfully realistic hands and feet. Make six sketches of your hands in different positions, for example holding an item, clenched or pointing.

2. Michelangelo also painted the *Doni Tondo*, a circular painting of the holy family, and he sculpted the *Taddei Tondo*, a circular relief sculpture of Mary and the Christ child. Design your own 'tondo'. Choose the medium that you wish to work in and the subject matter.

3. Michelangelo was also a highly-skilled poet. Use the letters of the word 'pieta' as the starting point for an acrostic. Illustrate this.

4. Draw the piece of sculpture, looking at the basic triangular shape that it forms. Try to make the drawing as accurate as possible.

5. Using clay, make a seated model of a mother and child.

TECHNIQUES

Although Michelangelo achieved wonderful things as both a painter and an architect, he always considered himself primarily a sculptor. He described sculpting as 'the art of taking away material'.

Stone carvers' tools have changed very little over the years and so the tools that Michelangelo would have used would be very similar to the ones still in use today. These would include metal-headed hammers, with the point and the pitcher to rough out the main shapes and take off large stone chips. Carving of any details could be done with a wooden mallet and chisels – a claw chisel leaves a furrowed surface, which is then smoothed with a flat chisel. The surface would then be polished using files and abrasive papers.

In his sculpture the *Pietà* Michelangelo achieved not only elegance and purity of line but also technical brilliance. This sculpture helped to establish his reputation.

Background

MICHELANGELO BUONARROTI 1475–1564

Michelangelo was born on 6 March 1475 at Caprese, Italy where his father was the chief official. He was sent to school in Florence where he showed an early talent. His father agreed to apprentice Michelangelo to the studio of Domenico Ghirlandaio. There he learned the art of fresco painting. In 1489 he was admitted to the School of Sculpture and very soon came to the notice of Lorenzo de Medici, who took him into his service. After Lorenzo de Medici's death Michelangelo worked in Rome. In 1501 he returned to Florence and was commissioned to carve the statue of *David* for the city.

In 1505 he was ordered to Rome by Pope Julius II but quarrelled with him over the work that he wanted and fled back to Florence. In 1508 he was reconciled with the Pope and returned to Rome, this time to paint the ceiling of the Sistine Chapel. He worked on this project virtually single-handed for four years. His last large painted work was completed when he was 71 years old, and he spent the last 17 years of his life as the architect of St Peter's in Rome.

The Census at Bethlehem

Time Line

1500	Vasco da Gama returns to Portugal after the first sea voyage to India and back.
1507	Martin Luther is ordained a priest.
1515	Pieter Brueghel the Elder is born.
1516	Sir Thomas More publishes *Utopia*.
1522	Ferdinand Magellan's voyage around the world is completed.
1531	Francisco Pizarro begins the conquest of the Inca Empire in Peru.
1534	England ceases to be a Roman Catholic country. Henry VIII becomes Head of the Church of England.
1540	The Society of Jesus (Jesuits) receives approval from the Pope.
1546	Pierre Lescot is commissioned to build the new Louvre by Francis I.
1558	Elizabeth I is crowned Queen of England. She restores Protestantism but tolerates other religions where they do not interfere with the state.
1562	French Wars of Religion between Catholics and Protestants.
1567	The Duke of Alva at the head of the Spanish Army moves into the Netherlands to suppress a revolt.
1568	Mercator's map of the world published.
1569	Pieter Brueghel the Elder dies.

The Census at Bethlehem *by Pieter Brueghel the Elder c.1515–1569.*
By courtesy of Musées Royaux des Beaux–Arts de Belgique, Brussels / Giraudon / Bridgeman Art Library, London.

QUESTIONS?????????

1. What is the story of the census at Bethlehem in the Bible?

2. Does the painting show many travellers arriving in a village and trying to find accommodation? Explain your answer.

3. Brueghel has based his town of Bethlehem on the local landscape that he knew in Belgium, showing the peasants of the region. Do you like it like this or would you imagine the scene to be different?

4. Would there have been snow on the ground in Bethlehem? Why has Brueghel included it?

5. Find the figures of Mary and Joseph. Where do the inn and the stable appear in this picture?

6. Identify the people in the painting who are going about their everyday life; for example the children playing, people building a house. Look at the picture and find a triangular table and people sleeping in a barrel!

TECHNIQUES

About 40 of Brueghel's paintings in oil and a few in tempera on linen have survived. He painted people and the countryside in all seasons, weathers and moods using a muted palette of blues, greens, greys and browns with an occasional enlivening touch of yellow or red.

ACTIVITIES

Individuals

1. Brueghel set this painting in his own time. Draw and paint a version of *The Census at Bethlehem* set in the present time. How would the visitors travel today? What would the weather be like? What type of inn would there be?

2. Choose one group of figures from this painting. Look at what they are doing and their involvement with one another. Carefully draw and paint them.

3. Look at the colours used with the red setting sun through the stark branches of the trees. Paint a background with a setting sun and use the branches of a tree as the foreground.

In Small Groups

4. Imagine that you own the best inn in Bethlehem. Design a poster to advertise its amenities and to encourage people to attend the census. You could set it in the present day, Brueghel's time or in biblical times.

5. Inns played a great part in a peasant's life. If they had any free time it was a good place to meet. Design and make a sign for this inn and choose an appropriate name for it.

Background

PIETER BRUEGHEL THE ELDER c.1515–1569

Brueghel was the last and possibly the greatest of the early artists from the Netherlands. There is an argument over the spelling of his name as he signed it both 'Bruhel' and 'Brueghel'. He founded a family of Flemish painters of which he was undoubtedly the most distinguished.

The date of his birth and details of his early training are uncertain, but he was certainly influenced by the work of Hieronymus Bosch.

He became a master of the Antwerp Guild in 1551 and he travelled extensively in Italy. He married the daughter of the painter P Coecke van Adst in 1563 and then moved from Antwerp to Brussels.

He had a sympathetic interest in the land and the people who worked close to it. *Peasant Wedding Feast* provides a detailed close-up of the peasants' happier times. He also used everyday sayings and proverbs to draw morals about the varied conditions of humanity. He died in 1569.

The Supper at Emmaus

Time Line

1573 — Michelangelo Merisi is born near Milan. He takes the name Caravaggio about 20 years later.

1574 — The Wars of Religion are renewed in France.

1576 — The provinces of the Netherlands unite to drive out the Spaniards.

1582 — Calendar reforms are commissioned by Pope Gregory XIII.

1587 — Execution of Mary, Queen of Scots for conspiracy against Queen Elizabeth I.

1588 — The English fleet defeat the Spanish Armada, aided by strong gales.

1589 — The Bourbon dynasty in France is founded by Henry IV.

1592 — Caravaggio moves to Rome.

1593 — Delft enamelware is produced.

1598 — Legal recognition is afforded to the Huguenots of France by the Edict of Nantes.

1603 — Elizabeth I dies and James I of the House of Stuart is crowned King of England.

1605 — Part I of *Don Quixote* is published by Miguel Cervantes.

1606 — Caravaggio kills an opponent over an incident during a tennis match. He is wounded but flees to Naples.
Guy Fawkes is executed for his part in the Gunpowder Plot (the attempt to blow up Parliament).

1610 — Henry IV of France is assassinated.
Galileo uses the telescope for astronomy.
Caravaggio dies of a fever at Port Ecole.

Background

MICHELANGELO CARAVAGGIO 1573–1610

Caravaggio was one of the most influential painters of the seventeenth century. He was a rebel, outside society's normal conventions. His short but tempestuous career was marked by disputes with both his patrons and the law and a series of acts of physical violence culminating in murder.

He was trained originally as a still-life painter and often included such details in his paintings. He had a very violent temper which led to disaster in 1606 when he became involved in a fierce fight during a tennis match over the non-payment of a wager. He was badly wounded but his opponent Ranuccio Tommasconi subsequently died from Caravaggio's attack.

Caravaggio fled from Rome and spent the next four years travelling from Naples to Malta, Syracuse, Messina and Palermo. He completed paintings in each town, his fame enabling him to be paid well for the work that he did. Finally he died of a fever in 1610 aged 38 at Port Ecole, 80 miles north of Rome. He had been hoping to receive a pardon and to be able to return to papal territory to rejoin his friends and patrons.

TECHNIQUES

Caravaggio was an extraordinary character. His career was punctuated by disputes with his patrons over his rather unconventional approach to religious themes.

He created a new vocabulary in art, his work being marked by naturalism sometimes of a brutal nature but mainly by his use of chiaroscuro. His figures are strikingly lit against deep black shadows. They stand out in prominent relief against their backgrounds.

Caravaggio was also one of the key figures in the development of still-life painting.

ACTIVITIES

Individuals

1. The text from the Bible upon which this picture is based reads: 'Then their eyes were opened, and they recognised him' (Luke 24: 31). Read the appropriate text and sketch a version of this moment. Do not copy Caravaggio's painting.

2. Caravaggio placed his figures against dark backgrounds to heighten the drama taking place. Paint a portrait of either one or two people at a dramatic moment, placing them against a dark background.

3. Arrange a basket of fruit or an assortment of different food items. Observe them carefully and draw what you see.

In Small Groups

4. Caravaggio committed a murder. Design a 'wanted poster' including a picture of what he may have looked like, a description, a reward and any other details that you feel may be necessary.

5. The artist was also made a Knight of Malta on 14 July 1608. This was the oldest order of chivalry founded to protect pilgrims travelling to Jerusalem. Design a symbol that could be used by the Knights of Malta. Find out what the Maltese cross looks like.

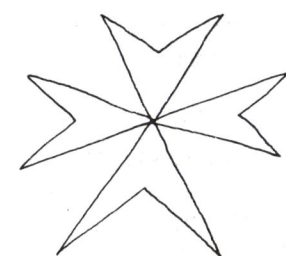

The Supper at Emmaus by Michelangelo Caravaggio 1573–1610.
By courtesy of The National Gallery, London / Bridgeman Art Library, London.

QUESTIONS?

1. What are the names of the disciples shown here? Look in the New Testament, Luke 24: 13–35.

2. The disciple on the right is wearing a scallop shell which is the symbol of the pilgrim. Find the names of two famous places that people make pilgrimages to today.

3. How is the shape and construction of the chair on the left different from chairs in modern homes?

4. Imagine speech bubbles for the four people portrayed here. What would they be saying?

5. The fruit and other things on the table are symbolic items, for example the bread and wine are symbols of the Eucharist. What are the main Christian symbols?

The Finding of the Young Saviour in the Temple

Time Line

1827	William Holman Hunt is born. *The Evening Standard* newspaper is published in London for the first time.
1829	The first police force is set up by Sir Robert Peel.
1833	Slavery abolished in the British Empire.
1844	The Co-operative Society is formed in Rochdale.
1851	London's Crystal Palace houses the Great Exhibition.
1853	The Crimean War starts.
1859	Charles Darwin publishes his *Origin of Species*.
1865	Antiseptic surgery is introduced by Joseph Lister.
1867	Volume 1 of *Das Kapital* is completed by Karl Marx.
1882	Robert Koch isolates the tuberculosis bacillus.
1883	The machine gun is invented by Hiram Maxim.
1898	The Curies discover radium.
1901	The first message is sent over Marconi's transatlantic wireless telegraph.
1903	The first aeroplane flight is made by the Wright brothers.
1905	The Theory of Relativity is presented by Einstein.
1909	The first aeroplane flight across the English Channel by Blériot.
1910	*The Firebird* by Stravinsky is performed. Union of South Africa is formed. William Holman Hunt dies.

Background

WILLIAM HOLMAN HUNT 1827–1910

William Holman Hunt joined forces with Dante Gabriel Rossetti and John Millais to form the PRB, the Pre-Raphaelite Brotherhood.

The group was attacked by the art establishment as it was seen to be setting itself up as better than Raphael.

They were defended by the critic John Ruskin in *The Times* for choosing to 'draw what they see irrespective of any conventional rules of picture making, as artists did before Raphael's time... there has been nothing in art so earnest as these pictures since Dürer.'

QUESTIONS?????????

1. What details of life at the time of Jesus can be found in the painting?

2. Compare the books that you are used to and the books that are depicted here. How are they different? Find some examples of Jewish writing and compare them to the alphabet that you know.

3. Where in the painting is there a beggar and a wooden cross, both symbols of Jesus' later life?

4. Are there examples of musical instruments in this picture? Describe them.

5. What would Jesus' mother Mary most likely be saying to him in the painting, having found him after he had wandered off?

ACTIVITIES

Individuals

In Small Groups

1. Look at the circular pattern on the Temple doors behind the Holy Family. Design a pattern with an oriental feel, within a circle.

2. Use the circle pattern as a repeating design on paper. Print the pattern using either a block or a screen. Blocks could be made from strong cardboard, vegetables or polystyrene.

3. Design a scroll of the type held by the priests in the picture. Write and illustrate this particular story from the New Testament on it.

4. Use a member of the class as a model and draw him or her in a seated position. These figures could be painted if required, cut out and mounted together to make a group collage.

5. Make a model in clay of a seated figure. An armature should not be necessary. Pay particular attention to the positioning of the limbs and also to any draped material on and around the figure.

The Finding of the Young Saviour in the Temple *by William Holman Hunt 1827–1910.*
By courtesy of Birmingham City Museums and Art Gallery / Bridgeman Art Library, London.

TECHNIQUES

Holman Hunt painted many biblical scenes, trying to achieve the Pre-Raphaelite ideals of serious moral content, direct study from nature and an authentic historical approach. His painting style was minutely detailed and he used straight compositional lines and bright, sometimes crude, colours.

The Yellow Christ

Time Line

1848 — Paul Gauguin is born in Paris.

1852 — Louis Napoleon Bonaparte comes to power in France.

1853 — Vincent Van Gogh is born in Groot Zundert, Netherlands.
The Crimean War starts.

1857 — Louis Pasteur begins his study of fermentation.

1869 — The opening of the Suez Canal, built by Ferdinand de Lesseps.

1871 — Giuseppe Verdi completes the opera *Aida*. A revolutionary government is set up in Paris by the Paris Commune.

1876 — The four-stroke internal combustion engine is developed by Nikolaus Otto.

1877 — Rodin's sculpture is exhibited in Paris.

1882 — *Parsifal* is produced by Wagner. Germany, Italy and Austria-Hungary form the Triple Alliance.

1884 — The steam turbine is developed by Charles Parsons.

1890 — The all-steel bridge is built across the Firth of Forth.
Vincent van Gogh commits suicide in Aures sur Oise, France.

1893 — Tchaikovsky composes the *Symphonie Pathétique*.

1896 — Cézanne paints the *Lake of Annecy*.

1899 — The Second Boer War starts in South Africa.

1900 — Freud's controversial *Interpretation of Dreams* is made public.
Coca-Cola arrives in Britain from America.

1903 — Gauguin dies in Arauna, Marquesas Islands.

The Yellow Christ *by Paul Gauguin 1848–1903. By courtesy of Albright Knox Art Gallery, Buffalo, New York / Bridgeman Art Library, London.*

QUESTIONS

1. Look at the colours used in the background. What season does this painting depict and what details suggest this?

2. Gauguin used the local Breton women at the foot of the cross, dressed in their traditional peasant costume. Do the figures fit well into this picture? Why?

3. Find the detail of the sailor climbing over a wall. This symbol was probably meant to give a sense of continuing daily life in the face of tragedy. Does it succeed?

4. The background shows the village of Pont Aven in Brittany, France. Is this a surprise? What should the background be of?

5. The painting is divided into three distinct areas (foreground, middle ground and background) by two horizontals. Find these areas on the picture and discuss them with a partner.

ACTIVITIES

Individuals

1. Make a painting of a landscape in three distinctly separate areas. Put a village in the background, some people performing an activity in the middle ground, and three large figures in the foreground.

2. Gauguin often wrote the title of his painting on the picture, incorporating it as part of the design. Design a title which would be suitable for use on *The Yellow Christ*.

In Small Groups

3. Gauguin called his house at Hivasa in the Marquesas 'Maison de Jouir' (the House of Pleasure) and he carved a door-frame for it with faces, flowers and curving stems as a pattern. Design a door frame for your classroom using the template on page 31. It could be designed and assembled in sections using bright colours. Gauguin included various sayings on his. One was 'Soyez amoureuses et vous serez heureuses' (Love and you will be happy). Discuss and decide upon the sayings to be used on your door frame.

4. Using a cross, design a pattern to be used as a repeating motif on textiles. Use only three colours.

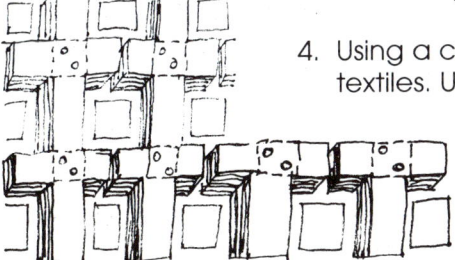

TECHNIQUES

Gauguin painted with large unbroken areas of colour. In his earlier paintings in Brittany these areas would often be separated by dark lines as in this painting, but later in his Tahitian paintings he would often first butt one colour up against another with no dark line between.

Two comments made by Paul Gauguin sum up his inspiration:

'A deep feeling can be interpreted instantly; dream over it, seek its simplest shape.'

'I have decided on Tahiti ... and I hope to cultivate my art there in the wild and primitive state.'

The Yellow Christ expressed Gauguin's own feelings about religion in a non-realist, distinctive manner using bold colours and outlines. He often added wax to his paints to give them smoothness and extra flow and the paint was usually applied thinly. During his Tahiti period he often painted on sackcloth or unprimed hessian, partly from an economic necessity but also because he liked the texture and surface weave.

Background

PAUL GAUGUIN 1848–1903

Gauguin's career was very varied. He became a successful stockbroker in Paris, painting in his spare time.

He believed that he was financially secure and in 1883 gave up his job to paint full-time. Despite some success he soon found himself very poor.

In 1891 he moved to Tahiti, which formed the inspiration for the majority of his work. He evolved a simplified non-naturalistic style, placing much emphasis on the use of flat, bright colours surrounded by black lines. He believed that an artist 'must synthesise his impressions and paint from memory, rather than depict events of surroundings directly'.

21

The Resurrection, Cookham

Time Line

1891 Stanley Spencer is born in Cookham on 30 June.

1892 Rudolph Diesel patents the diesel engine.

1900 International Exhibition opens in Paris.

1901 King Edward VII accedes to the throne of England.

1903 Henry Ford forms the Ford Motor Company in Detroit, America.

1911 Amundsen reaches the South Pole.

1912 The *Titanic* hits an iceberg and sinks.

1913 Cubism is banned at the Salon d'Automne exhibition of art.

1914 The First World War begins.

1918 End of the First World War. Stanley Spencer is appointed an official war artist.

1920 First radio transmissions.

1922 Mussolini comes to power in Rome.

1926 General Strike in Britain.

1927 The first talking film *The Jazz Singer* is released in America.

1936 Edward VIII abdicates and is succeeded by his brother, George VI.

1939 The Second World War begins.

1945 The Second World War ends.

1948 The state of Israel is born.

1953 Mount Everest is climbed for first the time.

1959 Stanley Spencer is knighted on 7 July and dies of cancer in December.

Background

STANLEY SPENCER 1891–1959

Stanley Spencer was one of the most original modern British artists. He had strong religious feelings that influenced his work. He was born in the Thames-side village of Cookham and made it a setting for many of his biblical and figure paintings. His painting of the Resurrection was set in Cookham churchyard.

A patriotic man, he was greatly influenced by his experiences in the First World War and by the women he married (Hilda Carline in 1925, and after their divorce, Patricia Preece in 1937). Spencer's training (at the Slade School) consisted almost entirely of pencil drawing from life and from antique casts, strongly based on form. This academic mastery was a typical Slade trademark. Spencer became a member of the Royal Academy in 1932, but later resigned in protest when two of his paintings were rejected. He became an official war artist in 1918, and again in 1940. He rejoined the Royal Academy in 1950 and was knighted on 7 July 1959. He died of cancer at Cookham in December 1959.

QUESTIONS

1. Along the wall of the church is a row of prophets from the Bible. Find and identify Moses.

2. What is unusual about the shapes of some of the gravestones?

3. Find the boat near the river bank in the painting.

4. Spencer painted himself twice in this picture lying on the right and standing naked between two tombstones. His wife Hilda was portrayed lying in the fenced tomb and smelling a flower. Can you find these portraits?

ACTIVITIES

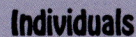 **Individuals**

1. This painting is on a grand scale being 2.74m x 5.48m. Choose a small section of it and draw it. Looking through a study frame will help.

2. Look at the many different flowers drawn. Try to paint accurately from life any plant or flower material available. Do not use a pencil to sketch but paint the image using a fine brush and a light colour.

3. Moses is represented here holding the Ten Commandments. Find out about them. Write them in your own words carefully in pen and ink. Add a decorated first letter to each commandment and a decorated border.

In Small Groups

4. Design a gravestone with an epitaph.

5. Paint a picture of people waking up. Look at how people stretch. How do they yawn? Do they rub their eyes? Include at least three figures in your painting.

The Resurrection, Cookham 1923–27 by Stanley Spencer 1891–1959.
By courtesy of The Tate Gallery, London / Bridgeman Art Library, London.

TECHNIQUES

The critic of *The Times* called this painting 'the most important picture painted by an English artist in the present century'. It was bought for the National Collection for £1000 as soon as it was exhibited.

Stanley Spencer was a meticulous craftsman and an isolated eccentric untouched by the modern trends in art. He had an extraordinary imagination and many of his pictures had a religious theme but often were set in Cookham Village, where he was born and spent most of his life. This painting is of the Resurrection of Man at the Last Judgement, but unlike traditional paintings of the subject, there is little indication of damnation or of suffering. Spencer spoke of this painting: 'No one is in a hurry in this painting ... in the main they resurrect to such a state of joy that they are content ... to remain where they have resurrected ...'.

The Sacrament of the Last Supper

Time Line

1904	Salvador Dali is born on 11 May.
1909	Bleriot flies across the Channel by aeroplane.
1914–18	The First World War.
1922	Tutankhamen's tomb is discovered.
1926	First television tests by John Logie Baird.
1933	Adolf Hitler becomes Chancellor of Germany.
1939–45	The Second World War.
1948	The state of Israel is born.
1952	The first hydrogen bomb is tested.
1955	Commercial television begins in Britain.
1960	Theodore Maiman develops the laser.
1961	Yuri Gagarin is the first man in space.
1966	Barclaycard, the first British credit card, is introduced.
1969	The first men land on the moon.
1977	The Space Shuttle makes its maiden test flight.
1979	The Soviet Union invades Afghanistan.
1981	The compact disc is launched.
1982	The Falklands War between Britain and Argentina.
1986	Nuclear disaster at Chernobyl, Russia.
1987	Van Gogh's *Sunflowers* is sold for £24 750 000.
1989	Salvador Dali dies.

Background

SALVADOR DALI 1904–1989

Salvador Dali was born in 1904 in Figueras, Spain. He was famous and notorious for his eccentric and extravagant statements and behaviour.

Dali joined the Surrealist movement in Paris in 1929 and was involved in the making of the Surrealist films *Le Chien Andalore* and *L'Age d'or* with Luis Buñuel. Dali himself pronounced the end of his influential yet bizarre period in 1939 when he said, "The two worst things that can happen to an ex-Surrealist today are firstly to become a mystic, and secondly to know how to draw. Both these forms of vigour have lately befallen me at one and the same time."

He was involved in many differing branches of the arts. He designed jewellery, stage sets, book illustrations and he was also the author of several books. His publications include *Diary of a Genius* written in 1966 and his *Unspeakable Confessions* in 1976. Dali was awarded one of Spain's highest decorations in 1964. During a fire at his home in 1982 he was severely burned. He died in 1989.

QUESTIONS

1. Look closely at the twelve disciples. What is noticeable about the two groups?

2. Who is the large figure at the top of the picture meant to represent?

3. This is *The Sacrament of the Last Supper*. What does the word sacrament mean?

4. Look at the background of the painting. Is this scene an interior or an exterior scene?

ACTIVITIES

Individuals

1. The two figures in the foreground are dressed in heavily-draped cloth. Drape some cloth or items of clothing over a chair or stool. Carefully observe and draw the items, paying particular attention to the light and shade created by the folds.

2. Using the same draped items, make a painting in monochrome. Try to make the painting as accurate as possible.

3. Paint a landscape using pale colours and include a beach, a small boat and reflections in the water. Try to give the impression of early-morning light.

In Small Groups

4. Model a kneeling figure in plaster. Mod-roc will give an interesting representation of folds.

Group or Whole Class

5. Draw and paint the portraits of 13 members of the class. Choose one to represent Jesus and the other twelve to be the disciples. Make a large frieze. Display the portraits as though they were seated around a table.

TECHNIQUES

Dali called his paintings 'hand-painted dream photographs'. They are notable for their minute detail, ingenuity, virtuoso technique and showmanship.

Dali included elements of Freudian dream symbolism in his paintings. His painting technique was brilliant. He portrayed fantastic imagery in a largely real, almost photographic style. The words that he used to describe his own technique included the following: superfine, deceptive, extravagant, extra-pictorial and super-plastic.

The Sacrament of the Last Supper *by Salvador Dali 1904–1989.*
© *Demart Pro Arte BV / DACS 1995 / Bridgeman Art Library.*

25

Coventry Cathedral – Baptistry Window

Time Line

1940 Cathedral Church of Saint Michael in Coventry is reduced to ruins by German fire bombs.

1941 USA joins Second World War after Japanese bomb the US Naval Base at Pearl Harbor, Hawaii.

1944 D-day landings in Normandy, France.

1945 The Second World War ends. The atom bomb is dropped on the Japanese cities of Hiroshima and Nagasaki. Japan surrenders.

1947 School leaving age is raised to 15.

1949 The world's first passenger jet airliner, *The Comet*, makes its maiden flight.

1952 King George VI dies and is succeeded by Queen Elizabeth II.
The first 33 rpm long-playing record is launched in Germany, by Deutsche Gramophon.

1953 Crick and Watson discover the secrets of DNA.

1954 Rebuilding starts at Coventry Cathedral.

1955 The first broadcast of commercial television in Britain.

1956 Traffic wardens are introduced. First nuclear power station in Britain at Calder Hall.

1957 Rock-and-roll becomes popular.

1959 Britain's first motorway, the M1 is opened.
The 'Mini' motorcar is designed by Alec Issigonis.

1962 The first hovercraft service starts. Benjamin Britten composes the *War Requiem*.
Coventry Cathedral is inaugurated.

Background

COVENTRY CATHEDRAL 1940–1962

On the night of Thursday 14 November 1940 the fourteenth-century church of Saint Michael in Coventry was reduced to ruins by fire bombs in the longest air-raid on any one night of any British city in the Second World War.

A cross was constructed of two irregular pieces of the charred roof beams tied together with wire and set up at the east end of the ruins. The decision was made to rebuild the cathedral as soon as possible. In 1947 a design competition was held for the reconstruction of the cathedral, open to architects of the British Commonwealth. It was won by Basil Spence. Reconstruction work began on 8 June 1954 and once completed the cathedral was consecrated on 25 May 1962 in the presence of Queen Elizabeth II.

The baptistry window was designed by an English painter named John Piper. He had gained distinction as a war artist and after designing the window went on to work on the decor of a number of operas.

TECHNIQUES

John Piper designed the Great Baptistry window and it was executed by Patrick Reyntiens.
   It is composed of 198 separate panes of stained glass. There is a border along the outer edges of the window in the style of the thirteenth-century artists who incorporated white or pale-coloured spots in order to prevent the colour appearing to spread. Light seems to blaze from the centre of the window but in the area behind the font, white, blue and yellow are included to give the impression of light and innocence.

ACTIVITIES

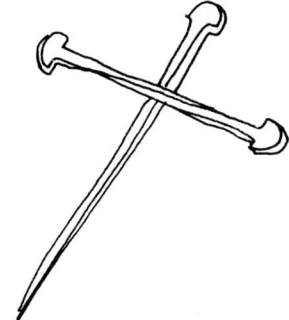

1. Design a rectangular window for the Baptistry Window using simple shapes and glowing colours. The windows could be displayed with plain dark paper shapes forming the counterpoint, as in the actual window.

2. After the bombing of Coventry in 1940, large fourteenth-century hand-forged nails that had held the roof beams together were found scattered in the debris. Four of these were fastened together to form the Cross of Nails. This became a symbol of reconciliation. Design a large cross to stand on the high altar, incorporating the Cross of Nails within the design.

3. Use the word 'reconciliation'. Design and use some letters. Paint or colour different areas around it.

4. Using clay, design and make a coil pot suitable to use as a candlestick for an altar. Research the diameter of available candles.

5. One of the most important works of art in Coventry Cathedral is the tapestry designed by Graham Sutherland. It is the largest in the world, 21.94m high and 11.5m wide. It is used instead of the traditional West Window and shows Christ with Mary between his feet.
Design and make a tapestry based on an event in the life of Jesus. Members of the class could each make a small part of one and these could be sewn together to make a large display.

Coventry Cathedral – Baptistry Window (1962) designed by John Piper and executed by Patrick Reyntiens. By permission of the Bursar, Coventry Cathedral / Bridgeman Art Library, London.

QUESTIONS ? ? ? ? ? ? ? ?

1. Find the system on the edges of this window that was used by the thirteenth-century artists in stained glass. Describe it and what it does.

2. Are the colours in the window arranged in any particular order?

3. Compare this to other stained-glass windows, possibly in a local church. Are there any similarities in the design?

4. Find out about John Piper. What other artistic work did he do?

5. The font in front of the window is a three-ton sandstone boulder from the Valley of Barakat (Valley of Blessedness) near Bethlehem. It is simple and natural in its appearance with just a scallop-shaped basin carved into it. Why does this fit well into the overall design?

A triskele pattern

- Colour in the triskele pattern using no more than three colours.
- Design your own triskele pattern – remember that it should have three 'sides' or 'parts' to it.

A street scene

- The template below shows a one-point perspective of a street. Complete the picture with other houses and details from a street that you know.
- Use the template to draw a picture of a railway tunnel, or a river valley. Think about the details that you could include.

VP - Vanishing Point

© Folens (copiable page)

A family shield

- Design a shield for your family. It should feature symbols that represent the jobs or hobbies of members of your family.
- Write your family name in the banner below. Make your writing as ornate as possible.

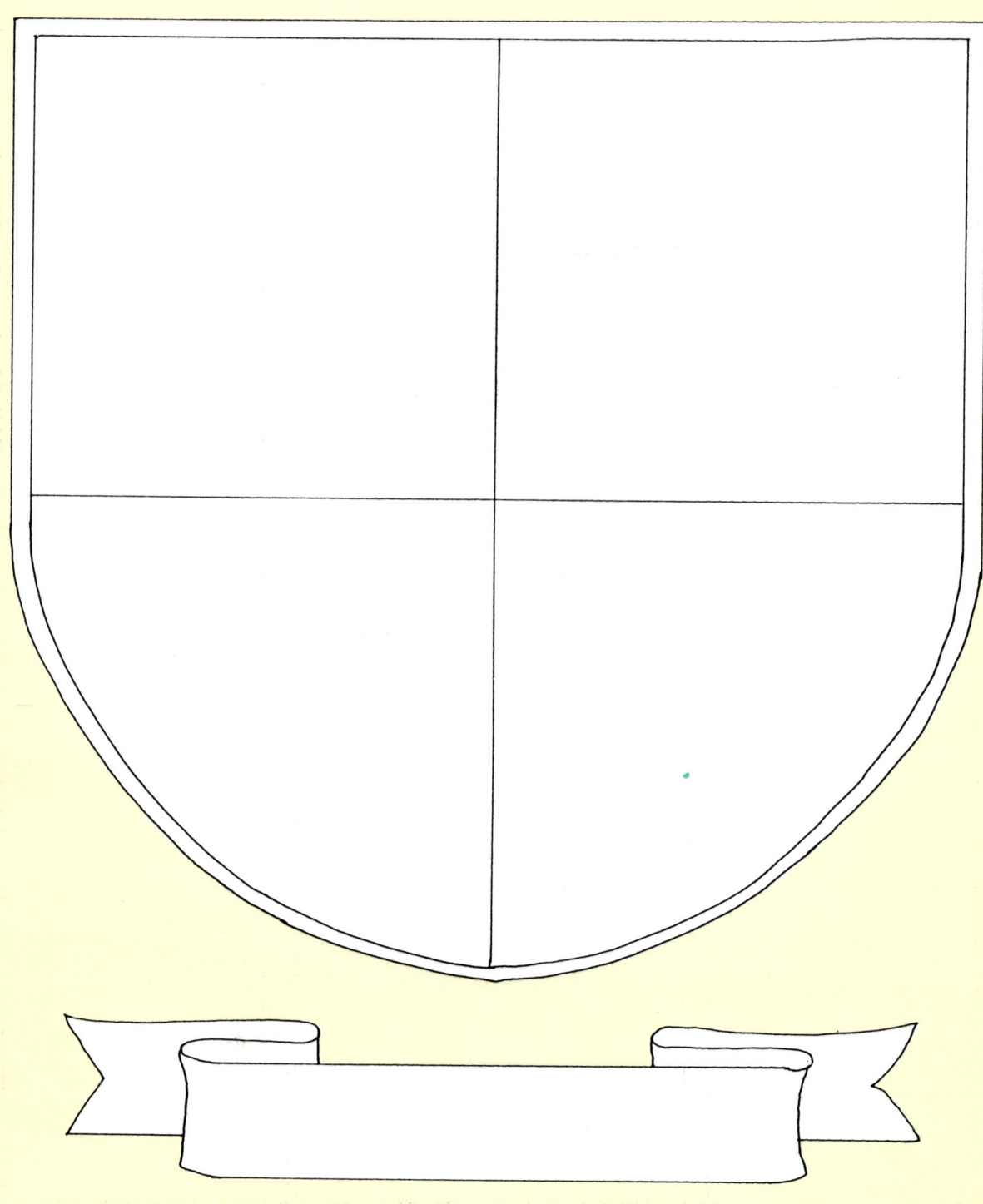

A door-frame pattern

- Using the door-frame drawn below, design a pattern for your classroom or bedroom. You may want to include animals or plants, or sports and interests that you have.
- Incorporate a message into your design such as 'Welcome'.

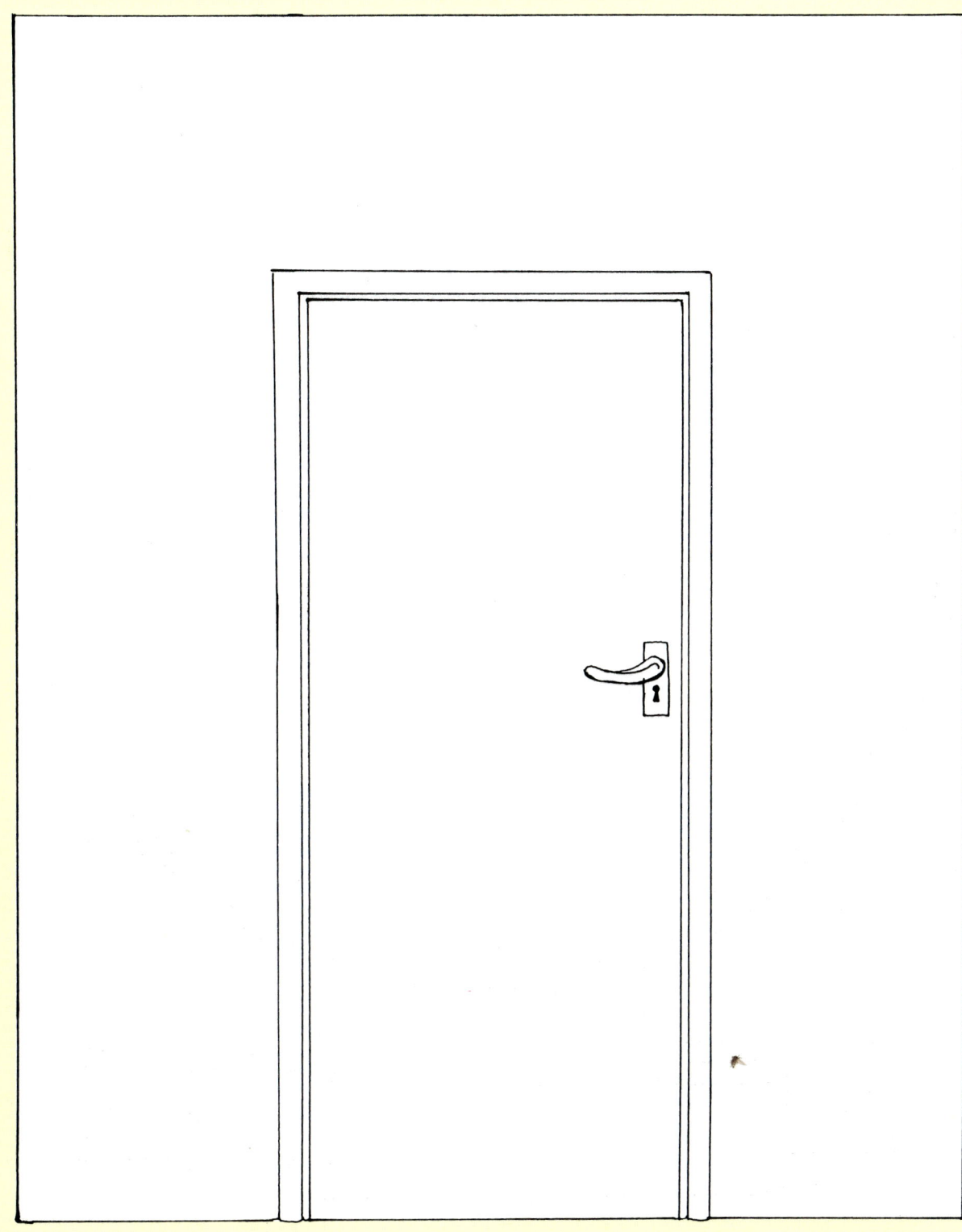

Glossary

Acrostic	A poem or word puzzle in which the first or last letters of each line form one or more words.
Antique	An item or style belonging to distant times.
Armature	A framework used as a base for modelling a clay or plaster sculpture.
Census	An official count of the population.
Chiaroscuro	Strong contrasts of light and shade for dramatic effect.
Eccentric	Unconventional in behaviour or appearance.
Epitaph	Words describing a dead person, usually inscribed on a gravestone or tomb.
Eucharist	Christian sacrament which involves the consecrating and consuming of wine and bread.
Evangelist	Any one of the authors of the four Gospels; Matthew, Mark, Luke and John.
Illumination	The decoration of a manuscript with colourful designs.
Meticulous	To show great attention to detail.
One-point perspective	A system of representing a three-dimensional view on a two-dimensional plane using only one vanishing point.
Parchment	Heavy paper-like material made from the skins of animals.
Perspective	The art of drawing solid objects to give the impression of their relative positions and size.
Reconciliation	The restoration of friendship between people after a quarrel.
Resurrection	Rising from the dead.
Sacrament	Christian symbolic ceremony, particularly baptism and the Eucharist.
Surrealism	Art form that tries to mingle reason with unreason, using chance effects, dreams, and so on, to create a new reality.
Tondo	A circular relief sculpture or a circular picture.
Triskele	A traditional Celtic pattern ('tri' meaning three) which involves a three-sided or three-legged shape.
Vanishing point	The point at which parallel lines appear to converge.
Woodcut	An engraving made on wood from which a print may be taken; especially used as book illustrations.